Micu—

I'm thankful
that our paths in
life have brought us
together as friends.
May God continue to
bless your journey.

Audrey
Alexander

DRAGONFLIES SAVED THE DAY

FIFTY-TWO WHIMSICAL REFLECTIONS, TRANSFORMING THOUGHTS, AND HUMBLE PRAYERS

by:
AUDREY ALEXANDER

authorHOUSE®

AuthorHouse™
1663 Liberty Drive
Bloomington, IN 47403
www.authorhouse.com
Phone: 1-800-839-8640

Published by AuthorHouse   2/16/2012

ISBN: 978-1-4685-4982-9 (sc)
ISBN: 978-1-4685-4983-6 (e)

Library of Congress Control Number: 2012902179

<u>ACKNOWLEDGEMENTS</u>

with heartfelt thanks to

Bill Albright

Paul Emily

Joel Stevenor

Carol Sowle

Richard Brendan

The salesclerk who changed
my attitude about my bathroom

All those who have walked with me on my path in life

The people at AuthorHouse Publishing

Dedicated with Love to:

My son, Charles

Sophia Ruach von Deus

— Reflection #1:

The color looked so pretty on the two-inch swatch in the paint store, so I bought a gallon of environmentally-friendly paint and went home excited to give my bathroom a face lift.

After hours of stripping wall paper (that came off in pieces the size of a corn kernel), I cleaned the walls, then primed them. Finally it was time to paint. As soon as the roller hit the wall, I gasped. This was a great color…for the bottom of a swimming pool! This color blue was at least three times brighter than the teeny swatch sample led me to believe.

What to do, oh what to do? Can't return paint; don't want to spend more money mixing this with another expensive gallon of white paint—so I guess I'll go with it and hopefully the color will grow on me.

When the painting was completed, I stepped back to evaluate. Nope. Not growing on me. And it wasn't in me to put in another sixteen hours of priming and painting.

Then I got an idea: I'll *make the best of it*. I bought a dragonfly stencil and several small bottles of acrylic paints and stenciled about a hundred little dragonflies in different colors all over one of the walls. I love it! Now I have a bright, whimsical bathroom! It might just be my favorite room in the house!

Think about it:

Sometimes the best we can do is choose to *make the best of it*—whatever "it" is. Approached with the right attitude, *making the best of it* can be better than expected. What's a situation in your life that, for the most part, cannot be changed but could be made better by adding a whimsical dragonfly?

Prayer:

Holy God, grant me the serenity to accept what I cannot change, the courage to change what I can, and the wisdom to add dragonflies that make me smile. Amen.

— Reflection #2: —————

For a while I had two dogs: Betsy, a small black 19 pound mutt, and Kaiser, a 75 pound German Short Hair. When Betsy was 18 years old, I adopted Kaiser when he was nine years old and no one wanted him. Betsy and Kaiser co-existed, so there was no competition for the alpha position. Betsy was her own woman. When I would call her in from sitting in the yard, I swear she would shake her head "no" at me. I'd have to walk out and explain it was time to come in. I don't know how to describe it, but she would roll her eyes at me, then walk into the house with a resentful demeanor and an indignant expression.

Kaiser, on the other hand, would be waiting at the door for me to let him in just in case I had a scrap of anything, anything at all, that he could eat. Kaiser would help a burglar carry out my curio cabinet for a piece of bacon. Whereas Betsy couldn't be bothered with any agenda other than her own, Kaiser was everybody's friend.

When Betsy was 20 years old, she died after a long struggle. I cried when my son and I carried her in a box with her favorite blanket to the vet for cremation. It was sad, but 20 years was a long, happy life for Betsy. It was a relief to see her at peace.

Then a year later, Kaiser's spine wouldn't send messages to his brain about where his hind legs were. He couldn't walk or stand. I'd come home to find him sprawled on the floor, unable to move. I'd lift his back legs up to help him stand, and my arms would be covered in his urine. It was time to make that difficult decision.

My friend went with me to the vet's office, and I sobbed and sobbed when I said goodbye to him. I swore I would never have another pet because I simply could not handle the heartache of losing another pet to death.

Two weeks later I went to the local shelter and adopted Jimmy. He's some sort of whippet mix, and he's a goof-head. But boy do I love him; and I'm sure he loves me because when he naps next to me on the couch, he has to have some part of him touching me. I'm glad to have Jimmy to love.

Think about it:

Find an animal to love. If you don't have a pet (or don't want a pet), look out the window and love the birds that fly over your yard. Or love the tigers, wolves, polar bears, and other endangered animals. Send a donation or write your congressmen to help save them. Or hang a picture of your favorite animal where you can see it every day. Just find an animal to love.

Prayer:

Holy God, move me to love all creatures, to respect all creatures, and to find some way, however small, to care for your creatures. Amen.

Audrey Alexander

— Reflection #3: ——————————

Wishful thinking: a desire to gain or obtain something that may or may not be realistic. _Optimism:_ the belief that if people would change, a positive outcome will occur. _Hope:_ the belief that there is at least a slight chance that a desire can be realized.

To illustrate the differences between wishful thinking, optimism, and hope: I hold in my hand an ordinary pen. I wish it were a magic wand. But I do not hope it is a magic wand because there is not the slightest chance it is or ever will be a magic wand. Nor am I optimistic it will become a magic wand if people would change their ways. But I still wish it were a magic wand. There are a lot of things I wish for knowing there isn't the slightest chance they will ever come true…such as looking like Jennifer Lopez. I'm sure lots of people wish I looked like Jennifer Lopez. Ain't gonna happen. So let's move on to talking about optimism.

I struggle with optimism. When I watch the evening news, I am anything but optimistic that people will change their ways. Of course optimism is healthier than pessimism. Studies show that continued pessimism wreaks havoc on the emotions, spirit, and physical body. And optimism is far more likely to bring about positive results than is pessimism. Even knowing that, I struggle with optimism.

But I am tenaciously hopeful. Hope brings God into the equation. I hope that God's grace will be experienced and shared between neighbors local and global. I hope that God's sense of humor will be received and shared. I hope that God's vision of social justice will be received and shared. There's a chance this desire can be realized.

Head's up: hoping for a specific outcome is not what hope is about. Granted, it is virtually impossible not to hope a loved one is healed or that a new job opportunity appears. But ultimately those are wishes which may or may not become reality. Hope, on the other hand, desires God's presence to be experienced *no matter what the outcome*. Hope desires an experience of God's comfort when sitting by an ailing loved one; hope desires an experience of God's patience while waiting for that job opportunity.

Hope's bottom line is for the highest good in any situation. Hope blindly believes God's presence will never leave us, no matter what.

Think about it:

Wishful thinking and optimism will get you far. Hope will get you through.

Prayer:

Holy God, my hope in you is never wasted because your Presence never leaves me. Walk with me and give me the spiritual strength to get through whatever life brings. Amen.

— Reflection #4:

In the movie *Les Miserables*, the protagonist, Jean Valjean (an escaped felon), is sitting as an observer in a courtroom. On trial is a man who is accused of being Jean Valjean. Obviously the man is not the one the court wants, but fellow convicts accuse the guy of being Valjean, and if convicted, the man will be executed. The real Jean Valjean must make a decision: keep quiet and keep safe, or save an innocent man's life and condemn himself to execution. Valjean stands up and tells the truth.

I am ashamed; I was unsure what I would have done in that situation. I'd like to think that because an innocent person was involved, I would have come clean. But those moments of equivocation brought my shadow side to uncomfortable awareness.

In another scene, Valjean, now the mayor of a small town, tells Javert, the police chief, "I order you to forgive yourself."

While this reflection cannot *order* you to forgive yourself, it invites you to do so. My equivocation discussed above was grounded in fear. Virtually all poor decisions are grounded in fear or ignorance. We are afraid we will lose something by telling the truth—be it our freedom as in Valjean's case; or our dignity; or someone's trust. We are afraid the truth will not get us what we want.

Ignorance is the other reason we make poor decisions. We mere mortals cannot fathom the far-reaching ripple effects of our choices, and so we often choose what seems good for ourselves in the moment...hence: imperfect choices.

Guilt lets us know we did something wrong; so guilt may serve a purpose for a while, but it is not helpful or healthy to let guilt eat at you for years. I have forgiven myself for feeling unsure about what I would do in Valjean's situation. And having reflected upon my shadow side, I have learned. That's what it's about.

Think about it:

What imperfect choices have you made that you still feel guilty about? Remember, poor decisions are made from fear and ignorance. You are imperfect, and imperfect people make imperfect decisions. One way to let go of guilt is to offer it to God. Confess your infraction, ask for continued wisdom to learn from it, THEN LET IT GO. Forgive yourself. It's time.

Prayer:

Holy God, help me learn from my mistakes and do better next time. Now help me forgive myself so I can let it go. Amen.

— Reflection #5:

New Year's Eve per se doesn't bother me; but when I hear *Auld Lang Syne*, I want to cry. Even if I hear it other than on New Year's Eve, I want to cry. Sometimes I do, sometimes I don't—but I always want to.

Auld Lang Syne is a Scottish folk song from the 1700s by Robert Burns. Literally translated it means "old long since," or as we would say, "days gone by;" or even "for old time's sake." *Auld Lang Syne* is sung to ease the pain of parting but with a promise of belonging and fellowship to take into the future. (See Wikipedia "Auld Lang Syne" for more info.)

Auld Lang Syne calls me to an awareness of time I will never have again. That makes me sad even if I don't want back some of the "days gone by."

To mask those feelings of loss and sadness with festivity is to dishonor the emotions associated with "what will never be again." So on New Year's Eve, I prefer to be alone—or at least not at a party. I am aware this is not a socially acceptable feeling, and I don't care. I prefer solitude on New Year's Eve so I can feel the loss of days gone by without having to eat pigs-in-a-blanket appetizers. I prefer to watch a movie, read a book, do a crossword puzzle, and listen to *Auld Lang Syne*—and I want to do that without a bunch of revelers reveling around me.

And that's OK because New Year's Day brings a brand new clean slate, a whole year of possibilities. Loss _never_ has the final word, even if it feels like it in the moment. But I've got to let myself feel the sadness of "old long since" so that I can wake up on New Year's Day with hope renewed.

Think about it:

Have you experienced any loss that you haven't let yourself grieve over? One cannot move through grief without acknowledging it and letting oneself feel it. That might take some tears, but the rainbow of new beginnings *always* appears.

Prayer:

Holy God, walk with me through tears and grief so I can more fully grasp your gift of new beginnings. Amen.

— Reflection #6:

My first pregnancy was difficult. For a couple of months I had to lie flat in bed so the fetus would not dislodge. After about two months, all was well, and I could function as well as any normal pregnancy allows. I gave birth to a healthy baby boy.

A few years later, I got pregnant again, but at this time, my mother was very ill and dying. I visited her almost every day, and those visits included helping lift her from the bed to the potty chair next to the bed, and then back to the bed again. At the same time, I was running after an active three-year-old. So lying in bed during this pregnancy was not an option. And at the end of my second month, I miscarried. But because of Mom's illness and imminent death, I didn't fully grieve the miscarriage.

Six or seven months later, it really hit me that I lost a baby. I told my minister about it, and he suggested I imagine the child as an angel with me. I liked that idea, and I even named my beloved angel "Brenda."

Brenda never leaves me. There are long stretches of time when I don't even think of her, and then something will occur, and I'll remember her presence. Sometimes I ask her for help with things, but she can be mischievous— like making me drive around the whole parking lot before showing me a space right in front of the store's door! I imagine her giggling and her little wings flapping. Then I start giggling. I love my Brenda-angel who is with me in a way she could not be had she donned a mortal body. Some day I'll see her and we'll giggle together.

Think about it:

Has someone you loved died? It's OK to continue talking with them; maybe the most they can do is listen, and that's OK, too, because some day you will giggle together.

Prayer:

Holy God, help me honor the lives of those I've lost by remembering them and by living life to the fullest until we meet again. Amen.

— Reflection #7:

I have very few irrational fears. I have the normal fear of spiders and snakes, and I experience vertigo when I'm more than three feet off the ground. But I have one irrational fear that I've had since I was six or seven years old.

A playmate told me that if I looked into a mirror at night in a dark room, Mary Worth would reach out from the mirror and kill me. I'm now 52 years old, and I have not looked into a mirror at night in a dark room since early childhood. When I go to the bathroom at night, I close my eyes when I walk by the mirror. I have no idea who or what Mary Worth is, but I don't want to meet her.

I know that the protective archangels of heaven are more powerful than whatever Mary Worth is, but what if they get called away for some cosmic purpose just as I open my eyes and look into the mirror? Nope, just can't risk it. Maybe some day I'll get over this, but probably not today.

Think about it:

Do you have any irrational fears? Whether it's time to do something about them or not, at least name them; admit them. You'll know when it's time to get help addressing them, but you can't address them until you name them.

Prayer:

Holy God, help me admit my fears, and remind me again that the power of your love is the strongest force in the universe. Amen.

Reflection #8:

There's a story about a blind man named Bartimaeus (Mark 10:46-52). He was begging on the streets when he heard Jesus pass by. Bartimaeus shouted, "Hey there, Jesus! Have mercy on me!" Some people told Bart to shut up, but Bart shouted even louder. Jesus stopped what he was doing and told Bart to come over and chat a while. Jesus said, "What do you want me to do for you?" Bartimaeus said, "Let me see again." And so it was done.

Seminary professors and theologians tend to focus on the double meaning of "see." The disciples never did "see" clearly; they were blind to what Jesus' life and teachings were about. But Bartimaeus "sees." Bartimaeus *understands* what Jesus is about. This is profound fodder for sermons, Bible studies, and spiritual meditations.

While I mean no diminishment or disrespect of what the author of this story intends, what has always struck me is that when asked, "What do you want?" Bartimaeus knows right away. I've thought a lot about this, and I still don't have one simple, pat answer should Jesus ask me "What do you want?" World peace? That my son be healthy? Enough money so I don't ever have to struggle? Truck loads of money so I can retire and be generous with friends and charities? Companionship? Wisdom? A bigger bra size?

I've thought about this for years, but unlike ol' Bart, I can't decide on one answer.

Think about it:

If God said to you, "What is the one thing you want?" what would you answer?

Prayer:

Holy God, grant me discernment so that I pray for what is good for me, for others, and for the world. Amen.

Audrey Alexander

— Reflection #9:

My son says my standards are too high, and it's not uncommon for people to accuse me of perfectionism. After insisting my standards are just fine and explaining that I don't strive for perfectionism, just flawlessness, I hear the annoying little voice in my head say, "Ya' want to think about what they said?"

OK, let's think about this. What's wrong with having high standards? It seems like mediocrity has become the norm, and that's OK with people. While many people are informed, well-educated, and intelligent, it seems like what used to earn a "C" in school now earns an "A;" and the grammar skills of even some professional academic writers indicates we have not done a good job teaching comma usage. Professional and academic writers should know how to use a comma. I see nothing wrong with high standards.

As to perfectionism: I strive for perfection in my sermons, liturgies, and certain other areas—*knowing full well I won't reach it*. But striving for it makes me do a better job than not striving for it. Alas, there is one area that this perfectionism-thing does not serve me well. On the very, very rare occasion when I play the piano in front of people, I feel I must perform perfectly because if I hit a wrong note, we can't be friends any more. It would be too humiliating to face you if I hit a wrong note. With only five years of piano lessons 40 years ago, it's virtually a given I will hit a wrong note; so I just can't risk playing in front of you. I know it's unrealistic to think I can play the first movement of Beethoven's *Sonate Pathetique* without error. (I'm decent at the second movement, and the third movement is out of my league to even try.) Admittedly the perfectionism-thing has me stymied in this area. It works for sermons, etc. because it helps me do my best; but playing the piano in front of people—nope, not gonna risk it.

Make no mistake: My standards may be high for other people, but I do not expect perfection from them. I could still be friends with them if *they* hit a wrong note. I guess this is one of those growing-edges for me.

Think about it:

Someone once said, "Perfectionism is the enemy of the good." In other words, don't discard something very good just because it isn't perfect. Is there anything in your life that you are a perfectionist about? Is it time to rethink that? Giving up perfectionist attitudes will free your spirit and psyche. It's worth it. Now if I would just take my own advice.

Prayer:

Holy God, help me to do my best and be satisfied that I tried my best. Amen.

Audrey Alexander

— Reflection #10: ————————————

Back when I was recently divorced, it was important to me to be at home in the morning and in the afternoon so I could be with my son before and after school. But this meant juggling four part-time jobs. Even with four part-time jobs, money was tight. Being a single parent was not something I was prepared for. And I wasn't particularly good at any of my jobs.

I was overwhelmed. Bringing home the bacon, cooking the bacon, cleaning up my son after he ate the bacon, cleaning the kitchen after frying the bacon, and working to afford the bacon was physically and spiritually exhausting.

One morning, after sending my son off to school, I started making my bed. But then I just sat down on the edge of the bed and cried. I prayed, "God, I'm beginning to doubt that you care about me! If you care about me—if you're even there at all—I want to see an angel in my bedroom before midnight tonight!" Then I wiped my eyes, finished making the bed, and went off to do whatever was on the to-do list for that day.

Sometime in the afternoon, a friend said to me, "Audrey, I got this poster, and I don't want it. Do you want it?" I said, "Sure. Thanks." I didn't think any more about the poster until that evening when I went to hang it up. I got a cheap frame from Walgreens, inserted the poster, and hung it in my bedroom. I stepped back to see if it was straight, and my jaw dropped. I just stared at the poster because it didn't strike me until that moment that it was a poster of an angel! There was an angel in my bedroom before midnight! I just whispered, "Thank you, God," and felt a sense of calm. To this day I am convinced it was not a coincidence.

Think about it:

They say (whoever "they" are) that angels are all around us. Sometimes when the going gets tough, we may start to doubt that. Consider naming an angel, and talk with that angel frequently. Maybe the most the angel will do is listen to the story of how your day went. Or maybe that angel will gently touch you with a sense of calm when you feel down. So why not give your angel a name? Let your angel remind you that you never walk alone—not even in the darkest of valleys.

Prayer:

Holy God, sometimes I feel alone and need a reminder you are near. Please send an angel to walk with me. Amen.

Audrey Alexander

— Reflection #11: ——————————

A friend of mine called to apologize. I had no idea what he had done that would require an apology, so I asked jokingly, "What did you do this time?"

He and another man had sung a duet during the Sunday morning worship service. While he was singing, the alarm on his cell phone went off! While he was singing, he reached into his pocket to get the phone, and while he was singing, he turned off the alarm. And while he was singing, he groped around for another pocket to put the phone back in. Amazingly he didn't miss a beat of the song!

But he called me that afternoon apologetic and embarrassed. He expressed that he felt he disrespected me and the congregation. I assured him that no apology was necessary because in my opinion, disrespect requires intent. He did not *intend* to disrespect me. His phone was turned off, but he learned the hard way that the alarm on his phone still works even when the phone itself is off. But there was no disrespect intended; therefore I did not feel disrespected. He appreciated my understanding, and our friendship is in no way diminished because of a rogue alarm on a cell phone.

Think about it:

Have you ever felt disrespected? Virtually everyone has. But not all disrespect is intended. Sometimes a person forgets to follow through on a promise; or someone inadvertently sticks his foot in his mouth and blurts out something that should not be blurted.

Look back on the times you've felt disrespected and ask yourself as honestly and as objectively as possible if the disrespect was intended. If it was, that's another issue for another day. But if no disrespect was intended, then please don't receive it as such. Receive it as an "oops" moment; receive it as an un-thought-out comment—and *we all make those*.

So maybe some feelings and some friendships can be spared if we take the high road and don't jump to feeling disrespected when none was intended.

Prayer:

Holy God, help me discern honestly whether disrespect was intended. If it wasn't, please help me let go of feeling hurt. Help me see it as an unfortunate mistake—something I make all the time! Amen.

— Reflection #12: —

Do you do any cleansing rituals? I do. Every August 18 I walk around my house and sprinkle salt while saying a continuous prayer that God protect my home and all who enter. And on December 31 I smudge. Smudging is burning *a bit* of sage to cleanse any negativity present; I burn *a bit* of sage while entering each room and say a prayer for blessing and protection.

Notice I said "a <u>bit</u> of sage." My son gave me a bundle of sage for Christmas one year, and I decided to save it for a cleansing ritual on New Year's Eve. Around 10 PM, I lit the entire sage bundle and walked through the house offering up my prayers. After a few minutes, I felt funny. I didn't think too much of it, and after an hour or so, I went to bed. As soon as my head hit the pillow, the room started spinning like crazy. It felt as though the whole house was spinning! So I went outside for a few minutes to get some fresh air, and I felt a little bit better. It was about 60 minutes before everything began to settle.

I told my son about it the next day, and he said, "Did you open any windows while you were smudging?" Well, no. He said, "Did you light one stick or did you light the entire bundle of sage?" I said the entire bundle. He busted out laughing and suggested that next time I light one little teeny tiny stick of sage and open a window in each room. He was laughing so hard he could hardly talk. Accused me of being a wanna-be shaman!

OK, lesson learned. Sprinkling salt is easier, but I still do smudging on December 31 to rid any residual negative energy.

Of course salt and sage are not magic talismans that prevent tornados or earthquakes; but ritual does invite positive energy into both the home and spirit. Ritual reminds us of the divine Presence. You can use whatever you want in your ritual—salt, sage, a candle, a sacred object, a gift from someone that's special to you, an article from nature…. Rituals connect our spirits with God's Spirit…worth taking a moment to do.

Think about it:

Why not give it a try? It may feel silly at first, but give it a try. Choose an article from nature or whatever you want, and hold the item as you walk into each room and say a prayer for protection, love, guidance. If you don't believe in such things, the absolute worst it can do is nothing. But I believe any invitation to positive energy is never wasted. Why not give it a try!

Prayer:

When entering each room, say something like, "Holy God, bless and cleanse this room. May all those who enter be grounded in your love." Amen.

— Reflection #13: ——————

If I could retrieve one word from colloquial misusage, it would be the word "awesome." The word "awe" comes from the Greek work *achos* meaning "fear." Awe is fear mingled with reverence and respect; a feeling produced by something majestic or sublime.

The Grand Canyon is awesome. The vastness of the universe is awesome. The birth of a child is awesome. My new shoes are classy—not awesome; the new flavor of bubblegum is tangy—not awesome; the latest video game is entertaining, but it is not awesome.

"Awesome" invokes an awareness of a benevolent power a trillion times greater than anything we mere mortals can produce.

I doubt I will be able to reverse the current and ubiquitous use of "awesome" to describe a cool T-shirt, but I've said what I need to say.

Now go look at the twinkling night sky and tell me that deserves the same adjective as a denim jacket.

Think about it:

Consider reserving the word "awesome" for only those times when the beauty and majesty of something brings you humbly to your knees in reverence.

Prayer:

Holy God, how majestic are your works! The beauty you have created is awesome. I bow in humility before your greatness. Amen.

— Reflection #14: —————————

Living a life of gratitude is a primary tenet in virtually all God-centered religions. Keep this thought in mind; we'll come back to it.

The Apostle Paul exhorts "Pray without ceasing" (I Thessalonians 5:17). Obviously we cannot pray with words 24-7-365. So how, then, can we pray constantly?

It is possible if we expand our understanding of prayer. If we define prayer as communication with God, then that communication includes not only speaking to God with words but also with emotions and attitudes (not to mention meditative and contemplative silence to listen to God).

If prayer includes attitudes, then living with an "attitude of gratitude" is possible 24-7-365. It takes practice, of course, and a good practice discipline is to say "flash prayers" of gratitude—using words at first. Start by saying thank you each day for something you've never said thank you for. Some examples: thank you for hot water for my shower; thank you for my pillow; thank you for forks; thank you for door handles. It's going to take some creative and observant thinking to come up with something to say thank you for every day that you've never said thank-you for. That means 365 different things each year.

If this discipline is taken seriously, then over time, momentary feelings of thankfulness will appear without words. Over more time, the feeling of thankfulness will remain…even on troubling days.

Think about it:

What if you lost everything you didn't say thank you for? Don't say thank you for toilet paper? You lose it! Don't say thank you for oxygen? You lose it! Even on the crummiest of days, there's a myriad of things to be grateful for!

Prayer:

Holy God, thank you for all the blessings of which I'm aware as well as for those I take for granted. Most of all, thank you, God, for your love which will never let me go. Amen.

— Reflection #15: ————————

For a couple of years I lived in anger, and every night I woke up from anger. My anger even had a color: a grayish-yellowish-brown; sort of like that piece of celery that gets stuck to the bottom of the recycle container.

One night, a few minutes before 3 AM, I woke up angry. I lay there for some moments and then thought, "Exactly how am I punishing _____ by waking up every night from anger?"

That was a turning point for me. It was time to forgive. Make no mistake: forgiveness does not mean what the other person did or said is OK. And realistically, it's virtually impossible to forget something that continues to hurt. But forgiveness ransoms the soul back to God; anger keeps the soul hostage in negativity. Forgiveness says *I refuse to let the other hold power over me any more.*

Of course there are situations in which anger is appropriate. Anger is a natural emotion and demands to be heard. How it is expressed is an issue, and anger as a way of life is an issue. So anger per se is not what this is about. But if you are living in anger like I was, then your spirit is held captive; your life becomes imprisoned. When you forgive, you free your spirit and give it back to God.

Think about it:

Forgiveness does not mean what someone said or did is OK. Forgiveness frees *you* from bondage to darkness. Look at it this way: anger is like drinking a cup of poison and waiting for the other person to die.

Are you ready to forgive?

Prayer:

Holy God, help me release my spirit from the darkness of anger. Help me move on knowing that the past cannot be undone, and also knowing that life is too short and precious to be held captive by anger. Help me, God, to surrender my anger to you. Amen.

— Reflection #16: ———————

Which is more important: light or darkness? warmth or
coolness? rest or activity? broccoli or chocolate?

The answer lies in *balance*. Balance is an important
concept in Buddhism. The Buddha teaches that neither
gluttony nor starvation, nor all work or all play leads to
enlightenment; the answer is balance. We need both light
and darkness, both warmth and coolness, both rest and
activity, both broccoli and chocolate.

Most people are out of balance in some way. Lots of
people are so busy that they don't have time to stop what
they're doing and talk with a friend who calls. Others are
couch potatoes whose only exercise is carrying chips and
dip back to the barcalounger. Still others cannot abide an
evening alone; they have to find someone—anyone—to do
something with. And others get flustered if they have to
interact with even one other person.

Of course we each have preferences. Some people prefer
daytime hours, others prefer evening hours. Some people
prefer to be warm, others prefer to be cool. Preferences
are fine; we're not talking about preferences. We're talking
about balance.

Life becomes imbalanced when extroverts take no time
to be alone; or when introverts refuse every social invitation
that crosses their paths. Life becomes imbalanced when
work hours take priority over weekend family hours; or
when chauffeuring kids to soccer practice leaves no time for
"Calgon to take me away." (For those of you significantly
younger than I, years ago, Calgon bubble bath had a
commercial that said, "Calgon, take me away"—meaning:
spend some quality time in a bubble bath after a day of

relentless activity. I suspect Calgon was more interested in selling its product than encouraging balance, but I digress.)

Virtually everyone is out of balance in some way. I work hard, and I rest well; but I don't play a lot, I don't do much for no other reason than to have fun. There are lots of ways to be out of balance, and the first step to repairing that balance is to name what aspects of your life are imbalanced.

Think about it:

Preferences are normal and natural, but take note and admit honestly in what ways you are out of balance. You can't do anything about a problem until you *name it*. Fear of naming an imbalance and not having time to think about naming an imbalance are red flags that you might be more out of balance than you realize!

Prayer:

Holy God, grant me the courage to honestly name the areas in which I am out of balance. Then, gracious God, grant me the strength to take a baby step towards a more balanced way of being. Amen.

— Reflection #17: ——————————

The mezuzah is a small scroll inscribed with verses from Deuteronomy. The scroll is rolled and placed in a case. "Mezuzah" is Hebrew for "door post," so the doorpost of a home seems a quite logical place to hang it. The mezuzah is lightly touched upon entering and leaving.

The first passage on the scroll is called the Shema: *Hear, O Israel: The Lord our God, the Lord is one. Love the Lord your God with all your heart and with all your soul and with all your strength. These commandments that I give you today are to be upon your hearts. Write them on the doorframes of your houses and on your gates* (Deuteronomy 6:4-6, 9 NIV).

When entering a home, the mezuzah reminds how we should act; likewise, when leaving, it reminds to observe appropriate behavior.

The mezuzah symbolizes God watching our coming and going—a Presence that never leaves us. (For observant Jews, there are strict rules about how it is made, from what it is made, and how it is to be hung.)

Think about it:

A reminder of God's presence every time we enter and leave our home is a wonderful idea. Consider hanging something above your doors or on your doorposts that reminds you of God's presence. It can be a mezuzah, cross, icon, something from nature—anything that reminds you that God is with you, and as a child of God, there are better and worse ways of conducting ourselves.

If you touched or saw a symbol reminding you that God is with you, would your drive differently? speak to a co-worker differently? rethink a questionable activity?

Audrey Alexander

Consider hanging a symbol of God's presence on your doorpost and touch it **_every_** time you enter and leave your home.

Prayer:

Holy God, remind me of your presence and love; help me live in ways that honor your presence and love. Amen.

For more Mezuzah information, confer <u>www. religionfacts.com/judaism/things/mezuzah.htm.</u>
Or just ask a rabbi.

— Reflection #18: ————————————

Just when were "the good old days"? The 1920s were notorious for organized crime, drugs, and alcohol abuse. The 30s had the Great Depression. The 40s had a World War and holocaust. The 50s had the Cold War and were what my friend calls "the decade of the charade." Everything is fine—as long as we don't mention wife abuse, mental illness, dysfunctional families, gays, and as long as someone is WASP.

The 60s were violent and turbulent; the 70s were a poor imitation of the 60s. The 80s were called "the Me generation"—when greed became a "good" thing. The 90s brought anthrax threats and red alerts. The new millennium has seen escalating violence, polarization, and the downfall of Wall Street.

So just when were "the good old days"? All days, all decades, all eras have both light and shadow sides. Sometimes we look back and romanticize the good parts and avoid looking at who was oppressed, hurting, and dying. We avoid looking because we were complicit in the shadow side either overtly or through ignorance of what was really going on. Other times we look back and see only the bad without acknowledging the work of those who moved society forward in some way.

More often my frustration is with those who glamorize how it was and spew negativity and condemnation about how it is today. Obviously there is a tremendous amount of work that still needs to be done for a more just and peaceful world. But there is also beauty in every day. Too often we forget to notice it. Medical advancements have saved lives that even 20 years ago would have been lost. More and

Audrey Alexander

more people are engaging an awareness of our precious and limited resources: *reduce, reuse, recycle* is no longer a slogan for left-wing hippies.

In the shadows of today's world, there is progress and beauty. We just need to notice it, focus on it, and quit romanticizing about the "good old days" when kids practiced ducking under desks to avoid nuclear fallout.

Think about it:

What do you consider "the good old days"? For me, it was when a real person answered the phone in the customer service department. I'll go farther than that: the good old days were when I could use my phone without consulting a 40-page instruction book. But here's a fuller version of the question: What do you consider the good old days? Why? What was not so good about them? How are you making your little corner of the world a better place today for a better tomorrow?

Prayer:

Holy God, help my thoughts and actions make my corner of the world a better place. May all our thoughts and actions be noble for our children's children. Amen.

— Reflection #19: —

Just a few minutes from my house is a restaurant that offers a HUGE all-you-can-eat buffet for under $7. I've gone there several times and have enjoyed it. But something nags at my conscience. How is it ethical for me to pay $7 and walk away stuffed while children a few miles from me go hungry—not to mention children in third world countries who die from starvation every day?

I've thought a lot about this and here's what I've come up with. Not eating at restaurants, including all-you-can-eat buffets, does not help those who are hungry; nor does eating there without a mindfulness of those who have little or no food help the situation. But eating there with an attitude of gratefulness sends out positive energy to the world. And feeling grateful inspires me to be more generous with my charitable donations. Being more generous with my charitable donations inspires me to view the world more compassionately on a daily basis.

I'm going to try something. Every time I eat at an all-you-can-eat buffet, I will donate five items to our local food pantry. That will keep me even more mindful of those in need.

My prayer is that some day soon, all children will enjoy dessert.

Think about it:

Boycotting and badmouthing all-you-can-eat buffets because others are hungry spews negative energy into an already hurting world. And ignoring local and global hunger oozes negative energy into the world. But appreciating what food is available, being mindful of those in need, being generous with charitable contributions, and advocating for those whose bellies bloat from hunger shoots positive energy all over.

Let your tummy be the catalyst for mindfulness and generosity.

Prayer:

Holy God, inspire those who have enough to be mindful of and generous with those who do not have enough. May some day soon, all have enough to eat because of justice, not charity. Amen.

— Reflection #20:

I love snow globes. When I was married, my husband gave me a beautiful snow globe with a happy snowman inside. I loved that snow globe...until I dropped it. Some lines of thought would suggest that there is no such thing as accidents. But I'm telling you: it was an accident. I loved it.

It's been about twenty years since I dropped it, and I still remember my beautiful snow globe fondly. I've never replaced it, and I'm not sure why. Maybe because it was a gift and simply buying another one just isn't the same as receiving a gift. Or maybe because the broken snow globe symbolizes on some level my now broken marriage—and I've just never wanted to get another one (meaning both snow globe and husband).

But whenever I pass pretty snow globes in the store, I remember what once was—and I smile. I smile because I remember both the beauty and the difficulties my now-broken snow globe represents. Or maybe I smile just because I like snow globes.

Think about it:

Do you have something that symbolizes a difficult and broken time in your past—or does the absence of something symbolize a broken and difficult past? Is it time to get rid of the thing that holds your memory there, or, as in my case, is it time to replace it?

Audrey Alexander

Prayer:

Holy God, help me learn from the past, appreciate that the past has helped inform who I am...and then help me let go of the past so I can fully embrace today. Amen.

— Reflection #21: ——————

When I was in kindergarten, I did everything I was supposed to do. I hung up my raincoat properly. I put the recess balls away properly. I was quiet during rest time. I did everything I was supposed to do, and I did it properly.

And then the most unfair thing in the whole entire world happened: for snack, the kid next to me got *two* graham crackers, and I got only one! Can you believe this travesty! I was not going to stand for this disregard of justice, so that evening I told my father about it. I pled my case better than the attorneys in a John Grisham novel could have done. I listed everything I did right and everything that dumb kid did wrong. I'm not sure what I expected my father to do, but it had better include a reckoning with the principal regarding a more justice-oriented distribution of graham crackers.

My dad listened to me, and when I was finished, he said, "Life's not fair," and went back to reading the paper.

Upon reflection, that actually was one of the most valuable lessons he taught me.

Think about it:

Life isn't fair. While we may know that intellectually, emotionally it's still hard to grasp, even as adults. But the sooner we embrace that lesson, the sooner we can move more freely through life. Life isn't fair, and there's nothing we can do about it except learn not to sweat the small stuff.

Prayer:

Holy God, help me keep a perspective about what is truly important in the grand scheme of things. Amen.

— Reflection #22:

When I lived in north-central Wisconsin, winters were very long and very cold. A few days after a particularly intense snowstorm, the roads were clear, and everyone was out and about as usual. On a busy two-lane highway just outside of town, I was driving towards home.

There was a micro-split second when I thought, "I'm gonna skid!" I have no memory at all of what actually happened, but the next thing I knew, my car was in the gutter facing on-coming traffic from the direction I had been driving. In other words, my car was in the gutter facing west next to the east-bound lane. The best I can figure is that I did 3 ½ spins before stopping...but I remember none of it.

Here's what's unexplainable to me: my car did not tip over; even though there was traffic behind me as well as on-coming traffic, I did not hit another car; I did not hit the mailbox just a few feet from where I landed. I didn't have as much as a bruise or a stiff neck. After the tow truck came, I drove home as if nothing had happened. No insurance needed to be filed because I didn't hit anything; the police were contacted but said they didn't need to come because I wasn't blocking traffic and no one was hurt. I just drove home perfectly fine as if nothing untoward had happened at all.

While I believe angels surround us all the time, I never fully subscribed to direct divine intervention...but sometimes I "got no other explanation."

Think about it:

Do you have any unexplainable experiences? How does one explain direct intervention in a specific case but not in all cases? That question is beyond my pay scale.

Prayer:

Holy God, there are things I cannot explain, things I don't understand. Help me to embrace the divine mystery rather than seek pat answers. Amen.

It's time.

A year ago I got Jimmy, my dog, from an animal shelter. He was about a year old and full of puppy-energy. Jumping the fence, barking at EVERYTHING, not coming in when I called him from the yard, jumping on me every time I put on my coat because he wanted to go with me, jumping on people when they came over, yanking on the leash, chewing "toys" that are not toys….

The other dogs I've had outgrew the puppy-energy, but I've had Jimmy a year now, and Jimmy has shown no interest in wanting to grow up, no inclination of wanting to improve himself.

I got the number of a dog obedience school and called them today. No answer. I will call again tomorrow. I must get a hold of them because there's no other way to describe this situation than "it's time."

Think about it:

What have you put off doing because you thought it would get better; or you've used the excuse "I've been too busy to address it;" or you've pretended that it isn't a problem?

Well, it's time.

Prayer:

Holy God, it's time. Help me to address the issue of _____ Amen.

— Reflection #24: ————————————

In the movie *City of Angels*, Seth is an angel that greets a person's soul at the moment of death. He then escorts the person into the Light. One of the souls he escorts is a young girl, maybe seven or eight years old. On the path to the Light, Seth asks the little girl what she liked best. Her response: pajamas! What an innocent, delightful answer: pajamas!

That got me to thinking: what do I like best? This is a "just for fun" question. Of course most people would pick a loved one; but other than a person, what do you like the best?

I like blankets; house shoes are a close second. Just thinking about this makes me smile.

Think about it:

What do you like for best (just for fun)?

Prayer:

Holy God, thank you not only for our loved ones and the major things in life, but also for the fun things, like _____ Amen. (And don't forget to smile when you pray this prayer!)

— Reflection #25:

When I was in my early teens, my mom and I were watching TV together, and there was a scene in which a scantily clad, beautiful woman was dancing in a cage in a swanky nightclub. I stood up, started dancing like the woman and said, "That's what I want to do. I want to dance in a nightclub. I want a boa to swing while I'm dancin' and I want a cage just like hers so I can dance all night long!" As I continued gyrating, I *expected* my mother to say, "Now that's nasty! You oughtn't say things like that! Sit down!" That's what I expected my mother to say.

Instead, what she said was, "Do you know how much energy it takes to move like that for eight hours? That's a difficult job. Those girls eat half a salad for lunch and then work out in the gym every day just to stay in shape for that job."

Rats. The part about working out in a gym every day rained on that parade. With all the dignity I could muster, I sat down and said, "Pass the chips. I have changed my mind."

What Mom did is called reframing. Reframing takes a situation and looks at it from another angle. It does not change anything about the situation; it merely looks at a different aspect of a situation and gives a different, broader picture of what is going on. Mom's reframing made me see the downside of the "glamour job," and calmly pointing out the downside of dancing all night in a cage was a much greater deterrent than telling me to be quiet and stop dancing like that!

Think about it:

In what situations are you at logger-heads with someone? While it is often very difficult to do, reframing can ease both sides into understanding another point of view. Reframing does not change the situation, nor does it demand anyone has to change his viewpoint. But presenting something from a different angle can help introduce new information that may possibly persuade. This is not the same as compromise; it is broadening an understanding of an existing situation. Again, it is often difficult to do when you "just know you are right!" But give it a try. Look at all angles of a situation. Reframe the situation. While it may be difficult to do, look at the success my mother had! I did not pursue a career as a nightclub dancer after all!

Prayer:

Holy God, give me an open mind so that I can objectively see more than one viewpoint in any situation. Amen.

— Reflection #26: ————————

What do you feel self-conscious about? In my teens, twenties, and thirties, I was extremely self-conscious about three of my physical imperfections. Even though I had more than three imperfections, for some reason, the others didn't bother me. But these three did. A lot. The "out-going" me was a masquerade; I was embarrassed by these three things that were "wrong" with me; these things could not be camouflaged with makeup or clothes.

And then something happened. I turned 40. I don't know what switched paths in my psyche, but all of a sudden, I didn't care; all imperfections became "so whats." I am in a much healthier emotional and spiritual state since I became able to say *so what* that A, B, and C about me aren't perfect, aren't up to society's standards of beauty. So what! Don't care. If someone doesn't like me because of a physical imperfection, then that's his problem. Make perverse and cruel fun of me because I'm not physically perfect. So what. Don't care.

Think about it:

It's often difficult in our younger years not to feel self-conscious about imperfections. But the sooner we can learn to say "so what," the sooner we will be emotionally and spiritually healthier.

Saying "so what" does not mean we shouldn't try to look our best or accent our assets; it doesn't mean ignore weight issues. It just means we're not going to waste energy feeling embarrassed because we don't meet the unrealistic standards of society's definition of beautiful.

Try this: look into a mirror and say out loud (for example): "My nose is too big. So what." Or "I'm too short (or too tall). So what." Practice saying **out loud** something you feel uncomfortable about, and then say "So what." I suggest doing this when you are alone; it'll go better, believe me.

It may take a while before you actually believe "so what." But the sooner you start working on this, the sooner life becomes a whole lot easier.

Prayer:

Holy God, thank you for thinking I'm beautiful just as I am. Amen.

— Reflection #27: ——————————

One evening I was at the St. Louis airport waiting to pick up a friend. Not surprisingly, I had to go to the bathroom. While I was washing my hands, I noticed a woman cleaning the mirrors and counters. I said, "I just want to thank you for doing that; it must be an endless job." She paused for a moment and said, "In all the years I've worked here, no one has ever said thank you to me." She smiled and said, "You're welcome!"

Now I make it a habit to thank any person I see cleaning a public place. Some people, especially younger ones, look at me like I'm weird. But most people sincerely appreciate being told thank you.

Think about it:

Consider saying thank you to those you see who are cleaning public places. Maybe they'll think you are strange, but maybe you will make their day and their spirits a little brighter.

Prayer:

Holy God, help me notice all who work to keep places cleaner and prettier. Then remind me to tell them thank you. Amen.

— Reflection #28: —————————

Can you be corrected without getting upset? Many people cannot. I used to feel hurt if anyone pointed out something I did wrong or said wrong. If someone said, "Hey, Audrey, you've got some mustard on your chin," I would act OK, but I'd go home feeling like the entire event was a failure and I was a failure and I couldn't do anything right. Fortunately I've done a 180 on that, and now you have to try really hard to embarrass me or upset me. It can be done, but you have to try really hard.

Anyway, many people cannot receive any kind of criticism, no matter how small. My father was one who could not. He had a long list of super-good traits, but he just didn't handle well anyone pointing out something he did wrong. One time he put seven or eight shirts in the laundry basket; Mom asked why there were more shirts than usual, and Dad said she'll never have to ask again because from now on there would be only one per week! I heard my mom ask him, and she wasn't accusing or upset—just curious. But Dad couldn't handle being asked why there were more dirty shirts than usual.

I know people who get bent out of shape when told, "You say 'you know' a lot when you're speaking." They get angry because someone pointed out a "character flaw"! They feel their personhood is under attack.

Can you be corrected without getting upset? Can you receive criticisms/comments/suggestions/questions at face value and not as an attack on your entire personality?

Think about it:

When someone corrects something about what you said or did, work on listening to what is being suggested instead of letting the words slap your ego. It is the ego that feels threatened when criticism hurts, and many people respond with anger.

Life will go much smoother if you learn to respond with "OK, thanks for telling me;" or "OK, I'll think about that." You don't need to agree, you don't need to change your being-ness on the spur of the moment, and you don't need to get angry. Just a simple, "OK, thanks for telling me" will keep the water smooth. It might just be that their suggestion/comment has merit...but you'll never know if you let that sensitive ego rule!

Prayer:

Holy God, help me to accept suggestions and criticism gracefully. Then help me discern if they have merit. Amen.

— Reflection #29: ———————

I know I am in the minority on this. But it bothers me enough to express it. Wherever I go, sales clerks call me—and many customers—"Hon" or "Sweetie." "Thank you, Hon;" "Thank you, Sweetie." I applaud them for saying "thank you." But I am not their "Hon" or "Sweetie." I am 52 years old, and the courteous address is "Ma'am." There seems to be an aversion to using "Sir" or "Ma'am" as a polite and appropriate form of address.

What's even worse is when someone does show the courtesy of "Sir" or "Ma'am" and the recipient of the courtesy says, "'Sir' is my father! Don't call me 'Sir!'" Or "How old do you think I am! Don't call me 'Ma'am!'" To reject the extension of courtesy is worse than calling an anonymous paying customer "Sweetie" or "Hon."

Sadly there seems to be a lack of simple common courtesy in today's world. Apparently common courtesy and the titles of address of "Sir" or "Ma'am" are outdated, archaic, and, for some people, insulting. How sad. How terribly sad.

I appreciate when someone shows enough manners to address me as "Ma'am." It's a title of respect. And to refuse that respect, even with a kidding tone, is, in my opinion, rude.

OK, I've said what I need to say.

Think about it:

Do you find it offensive when people address you as "Sir" or "Ma'am"? Why? Even if it does seem offensive to you, PLEASE do not "correct" the person who showed you simple, common courtesy. We have little enough courtesy and manners in our society without shunning what is offered.

I will continue to address people as "Sir" or "Ma'am," and I will continue to appreciate when the courtesy is shown to me.

Prayer:

Holy God, help me show and accept—with grace—common courtesy. May this small act make the world a better and more civil place. Amen.

— Reflection #30: ————————

In the movie *Diary of a Wimpy Kid*, Greg, a young boy entering middle school, struggles to find a place for himself among the popular kids. He fails miserably at wrestling, acting, and a host of other things. Finally he finds his niche as a "security guard"—the guy who walks home a bunch of kindergartners.

But then something happens, and Greg's friend takes the rap for something Greg did. If Greg confesses the truth, he's in trouble; if Greg remains silent, his friend is in trouble.

Greg's mom notices that Greg is worried about something and tells him, "It's our choices that make us who we are."

Think about it:

While most of the movie consists of middle-school humor, that line from Greg's mom is profound. Because we all make choices throughout our lives, it's a good reminder no matter what our age that "our choices make us who we are."

If we were mindful of the consequences, would we choose the same options that we pick when we are angry, afraid, tired, resentful, protecting our ego…? Probably not.

Prayer:

Holy God, help me make choices that reflect my relationship with you. Amen.

— Reflection #31: —

Do you have trouble keeping a secret? In my job, keeping people's secrets is expected. I've learned to keep my mouth shut. But some people simply cannot keep a secret. Sheldon, on *The Big Bang Theory*, gets an eye tic, then blurts out whatever it is he's not supposed to tell. That makes for some laughs on a sit-com, but in real life, it can have devastating and painful consequences.

Heads up—this is important: keeping secrets about abuse or violence or suicidal thoughts are NOT secrets that should be kept. If you or someone you know has talked about being abused, or abusing, or being the victim or perpetrator of violence; or if you or someone you know has suicidal thoughts: **GET HELP!** Those are not the kinds of secrets I'm talking about. I'm talking about when someone shares a confidence with you, can you honor that? Can you keep a secret? Or do you, like Sheldon, get an eye tic and just have to tell somebody?

Think about it:

If you feel the need to tell someone a secret, buy a stuffed animal and tell it. Or tell it to your pillow. Or whisper it ever so quietly in the shower. In other words, get it outside of yourself in a private and safe way. That way it won't feel bottled up in you. Much better to talk to a stuffed animal than to have betrayed someone's trust.

Prayer:

Holy God, let me never betray a trust; but let me be discerning when the secret is harmful. Help me, holy God, to do the right thing. Amen.

— Reflection #32: —————————

When's the last time you learned something new? Students get bombarded with new stuff every day, but those of us who've been out of school for a while may have lost the incentive to keep learning.

One of the best ways to stay healthy on all levels is to learn something new. It may take a couple of tries to find something you'd like to learn, but stick with it. Over the years I've signed up for French classes, Spanish classes, cooking classes, knitting classes, and bought a couple of "teach yourself Latin" books. I dropped out of all the classes after a couple of lessons, and my "teach yourself Latin" books now serve as coasters. But I kept seeking and finally found something that interested me: Quantum Touch. Quantum Touch is a modality of hands-on healing, and I love offering it. It took a while—years, actually—to find something that I wanted to learn about and keep learning about, but I did it. I am now a certified practitioner.

Think about it:

When is the last time you learned something new? No matter how old you are, it's never too late to learn. What if you opened the dictionary at random and learned a new word once a week? That would cost you nothing. And if you remembered only ten new words out of the 52 you looked up—so what! That's ten more words you now know than you knew before. Or sign up for an evening of learning how to decorate cakes. Even if you never decorate a cake after the course is over, so what? You learned something new. If nothing else, you will have gained an appreciation for those who do cake decorating for a living. Or what if you took an automotive class? Or a woodworking class? You never know what seemingly insignificant skill you learned in the woodworking class will come in handy on the "honey-do" list.

It honors God when we use our minds that God gave us.

Prayer:

Holy God, help me to love you with both my heart and mind. Amen.

— Reflection #33: ——————

Did you ever feel blue for no discernable reason? Every once in a while—not often, but every once in a while—I feel sad. And there's no reason for me to feel sad. I have a good job. I have a wonderful home. I have terrific friends. My son is doing fine. The sun is shining…and I feel sad.

I often counsel people that small doses of "poor me" are normal. Give yourself 24 hours to feel down in the dumps, and then intentionally pull yourself out of it. One of the best ways to do this is to help someone else. Sometimes I go through my closet and pick out two things to give to Goodwill. Or I make a special trip to the store and buy two items to give to the local food pantry. Guys, do a handyman project for a neighbor. If you can afford it, write a $20 check to save the Australian slime beetle.

The point is to do something for someone else even if you don't feel like it. Do it anyway.

Think about it:

What do you do when you feel down in the dumps? Whine? Take a mood-altering pill? Drink alcohol? There are better options. Helping someone else physiologically produces a "feel-good" hormone in our brains. I'm not making this up. People a lot smarter than I recommend this option. It's worth a try.

Prayer:

Holy God, pull me out of self-pity so I can more readily see the needs of others. Open my heart to appreciate what blessings I have, and then help me be a blessing to others. Amen.

— Reflection #34: ————————

In the first year I was married, I made some soup for dinner and wanted to keep it warm until my husband came home. So I poured it into a large Tupperware container and set it on one of the burners of the stove. Since I just wanted to keep it warm, I turned the burner on "low." About 20 minutes later, I noticed orange-ish goo beneath the bowl. So I lifted the bowl off the burner, except the bowl didn't come off the burner. Strings of Tupperware stretched from the burner no matter how far up I lifted the bowl. The strings of Tupperware would not tear. They just stretched and stretched until I had dozens of goo-strings about three feet long that wouldn't break. I don't remember exactly, but I think I stretched the goo-strings over to the junk drawer, got a pair of scissors, and cut them. Meanwhile little holes were appearing in the bottom of the bowl, so soup was oozing out across the kitchen. In case you haven't experienced this, let me inform you that Tupperware string-goo does not come off an electric stove burner easily. I bet it was two months before I got all the string-goo off the back burner. Oops!

Think about it:

Are you able to laugh at oops!es? Sometimes people can laugh at their own oops!es but not at the oops!es of others. And some people can laugh at the oops!es of others, but not at their own. Life goes better when oops!es produce good laughs. What good would it have done to beat myself up over this or for my husband to have berated me? Yep, better to laugh about it and buy another Tupperware bowl.

Audrey Alexander

Prayer:

Holy God, give me the grace to laugh at oops!es. Help me keep life in perspective by not sweating the small stuff. Amen.

— Reflection #35: ————————

My mom died in 1989. In 1995 I entered seminary. It was during my seminary years that my grandma said to me, "God took your mom; I guess he needed her for something." I nodded sympathetically because Grandma was expressing grief, but inside I was screaming, "God doesn't *take* people! God *receives* people! And what would God *need* someone for!" I was so frustrated that Grandma didn't understand the intricacies of theological discernment!

But I have matured. I have come to understand Grandma's statement to mean "I don't understand why my child died, but I trust that she's with God now." That's a profound statement of faith. We mere mortals cannot understand divine mystery, but we can cling to faith that God's love and presence are with us in this life and the next.

Think about it:

As stated above, I do not believe God *takes* people. The human body is vulnerable to age, disease, illness, accidents. At some point, our physical bodies will expire. There is no need for God to *take* us. What I'm betting my soul on is that God *receives* us, receives every soul without exception. I also believe that we are received in unconditional love. This means no one is "left behind." There may be a *hell* of a life-review, but ultimately we will all be drawn into the most powerful force in the universe: God's love.

Do you believe God's love is the most powerful force in the universe?

Do you believe in an eternal hell? If so, then you believe God's judgment is stronger than God's love. Think about why you do or do not feel the need for an eternal hell if God's love is the strongest force.

Prayer:

Holy God, I don't understand how things work, but I trust that your love is the most powerful force in the universe. Amen.

— Reflection #36: ——————————

In my line of work, people frequently ask me to pray for them. I have also frequently heard the phrase, "Be careful what you pray for, you might get it."

Because no human being can understand "the grand scheme of things," I put all my prayer requests back into the hands of God with the phrase "for the highest good." For example, "Please help *name* get a job at *place* for the highest good." If the job would turn out to be awful or painful, then I wouldn't want the person to get it.

Another popular prayer is "Dear God, I need more money." But what if someone had to die for you to get that money; would you want it then? Or what if you had to be in an accident and sue someone to get more money—would you really want to get richer like that?

Of course troubling situations will still happen even with "for the highest good" added to our prayers; the phrase is not a magic charm. Rather, it reminds us that what we think we want may not be what is best in the long run. It reminds us that we are directing our prayers to a higher power of goodness, not a divine vending machine. It also keeps us humble by acknowledging we don't–can't—know the long range costs and rewards of what we are asking.

Think about it:

Consider adding "for the highest good" to all your prayers. It humbly acknowledges that God is a lot smarter than we are.

Prayer:

Holy God, only you know what the highest good is. Help me bow before your wisdom. Grant to me only that which is for the highest good. Amen.

— Reflection #37: —————————

The Apostle Paul says in his letter to the Ephesians, "Do not let the sun go down on your anger" (Eph 4:26 NRSV). Overall I agree with that, but not 100% of the time. For example, someone says something you don't think is funny... yeah, let that go before the sun goes down. Or the toilet seat is left up—again...yep, let it go before bedtime. Or someone cuts you off in traffic...say bye-bye to that frustration before the day is over.

But, if someone lies about you at work; or your significant other and you have a *major* argument; or your neighbor erects his fence five feet onto your property...those things take some thought on the best way to handle them. Coming up with ideas while seething with anger is not the best time to come up with ideas; nor should major infractions simply be dismissed just because the sun has gone down. Situations of a major bent take time, prayer, and thoughtful reflection on how best to handle them.

Look at it this way: did you ever try to pick up dog poop in the yard right after a rain storm? Can't be done. You might get some of it, but soppy dog poop smears. Better to wait a few days until it sets and is more easily removed.

The same with anger. Yelling back at the lying co-worker, aggressively confronting, or secretly spreading lies about him are like smeary dog poop. Trying to address the issue while angry just smears the problem.

Talking calmly with the boss without accusation; treating the co-worker to lunch and asking gently what's going on; concluding that the lie is ultimately inconsequential and choosing to do nothing...options like that can be thought of only after time, prayer, and rational reflection.

Think about it:

One way to discern whether an infraction is worth stewing over: ask yourself, "Will this matter in one year from now? Five years from now?" After thinking about it, if it really isn't going to matter in the long run, then let it go. Try to let it go before the sun goes down. But if the infraction is something that has and will continue to cause harm, then think carefully about it before deciding what to do. That's going to take a good night's sleep with a lot of prayer. Addressing major issues in the heat of the moment is just going to smear them all over everything.

Prayer:

Holy God, help me discern what is worth getting upset over and what is small potatoes in the grand scheme. Then help me act in appropriate ways to address the problem. Amen.

— Reflection #38: —————————————

Affirmations and a show of appreciation make us feel good; the pat on the back makes our efforts feel worthwhile.

But what if you do your best and don't get affirmed for a job well done? Of course it may hurt our feelings not to receive that pat, but what we do with that hurt is up to us. We can let it eat away at our spirits…or we can begin to affirm others! Yep, that's right. Start affirming others more often, and over time, affirmations will come your way. It might be a long dry spell before they start trickling in, but making an intentional effort to frequently affirm others will alter the course of the energies surrounding you by attracting "affirmation energy" to come your way. This is an example of "what you sow, you reap." Start sowing affirmations to others, and you will reap a whole crop of ooohs and aaahs!

Think about it:

Gurus and bodhisattvas don't need the affirmations of others. They are spiritually mature to such a high degree that ooohs and aaahs are meaningless to them. But let's face it: the rest of us mere mortals are not usually that spiritually developed. We start to doubt ourselves and feel bad about ourselves if no one *ever* says "good job." For better or worse, most of us still need the occasional affirmation to keep our spirits up.

So start affirming others. Find something good to say about the job someone else did. At first this may feel like rubbing salt in your own wound—having to compliment others when you yourself are in need of compliments. But

Audrey Alexander

stick with it. Over time, affirmations will indeed come your way. "What you sow, you reap" was recited by someone a lot more spiritually mature than I, so you can bet it's true.

Prayer:

Holy God, give me the grace to affirm others, not just so I can be affirmed, but because it's the right thing to do. Amen.

— Reflection #39: —————————

When I was pre-teen, I told my mom I wanted to be a stewardess. She told me that stewardesses are nothing more than glorified waitresses; choose something else. In my early teens I told my dad I wanted to study Greek and Roman mythology. He told me that there's nothing to do with that information; choose something else. In my late teens I got a job as a part-time bank teller for the summer. Mom said I wouldn't be able to learn to do it in that short a time.

My parents were not trying to be mean or even discouraging; they were being realistic. But it sure felt discouraging. And unwittingly I carried the "realism" trait into my parenting. When my son was about seven years old, he told me he wanted to be a basketball player. I told him that neither his father nor I were tall, and chances are that he wouldn't be tall enough to play; choose something else. During his early teens he told me he wanted to be an engineer for NASA. I told him that NASA doesn't hire engineers right out of college, that one has to prove himself superior to other engineers before NASA employs; better plan to choose something else.

Like my parents, I wasn't trying to be mean. I was trying to spare my son from unrealistic expectations and heartache when dreams don't come true. But looking back, I'm sure that's not how it came across. I'm sure I came across as a dream-crusher, just like my parents. That's one of the things I most regret about my parenting. I crushed dreams. I am terribly sorry about that. If I could, I would do it differently because I've learned that nothing at all can be accomplished without it first being a dream.

Audrey Alexander

Think about it:

Nothing can happen without it first being a dream. Be mindful of crushing the dreams of others—as well as your own—with an *unhealthy* dose of realism. Be especially mindful of crushing the dreams of children. They will learn soon enough that they are not tall enough to play professional basketball or that being an airline stewardess is not all glitter and glamour. They will learn without having the dream ripped out from under them. Being grounded in reality is fine, but don't let *improbable* mean the same as *impossible*.

Prayer:

Holy God, help me dream dreams and encourage others to dream dreams that are pleasing to you. Amen.

— **Reflection #40:** ———————

In 1987, I gave my dad a book for Christmas called *The Book of Questions* by Gregory Stock (Workman Publishing: New York. 1987). I recommend the book for anything from chit-chat fodder to deep-discussion material. Because I love to ponder imponderables, I came up with three of my own questions.

- If you could get rid of all your physical imperfections, design exactly what you wanted to look like, and remain healthy throughout your entire life—but you'd lose 15 IQ points, would you do it? Why or why not?
- Would you allow both your arms to be amputated if it would save the lives of 1000 people you didn't know? Why or why not?
- Would you rather spend your lifetime with someone you loved deeply, but for the rest of your lives, you would never have enough money to even eke by; or would you rather have all the money you want for whatever you want but would feel loneliness every day of your life? Why?

Think about it:

Make up three questions and have fun discussing them with your family and friends.

Prayer:

Holy God, help me remember that sometimes wisdom is not in the answers but in what questions we ask. Amen.

— Reflection #41: ————————

As a Quantum Touch practitioner, the #1 excuse people who are interested in receiving a session give me for not scheduling an appointment: "I don't have time." Hmmm. "I don't have time" is patently untrue. We all have 24 hours a day to do with as we see fit. What "I don't have time" really means is "Everything else I have to do is more important."

Maybe that's true; quite possibly that's true. We all schedule our days according to what we deem is the most important to get done. That's true of every person every day. "I don't have time" is a questionable excuse because I have exactly the same amount of time per day as you do; what we choose to do with our time shows where our priorities lie.

Think about it:

How often do you say to people, "I'd like to do that, but I don't have time?" Do you really mean "I'd like to do it," or is that a phrase spoken just to please the other person? Is everything else you have to do really more important than what you rejected because "you don't have time?" Maybe it is; seriously, maybe it is. But be aware of your options. What could you skip doing and replace with something that you'd like to do?

Make no mistake: I use the phrase "I don't have time," too. Sometimes it's legitimate, like when I have obligations to complete for my job. But sometimes I am well aware that I use it as nothing but an excuse: "I'd sure like mop my floors, but I don't have time. I have to watch *The Mentalist*; I have to finish my crossword puzzle; I have to play *Text Twist* on the computer." Yes indeedy, "I don't have time" has come in handy when it delays housework. Just be aware that we all "have time;" we all have 24 hours a day. It's what we choose to do with it that exposes what we think is important.

Prayer:

Holy God, help me use my time wisely. Amen.

— Reflection #42:

One of the most frustrating aspects of ministry is when someone goes into the hospital, gets hurt, has an accident, feels ill…and no one tells me! Every year, one or two persons/families get angry at me because I didn't call or visit when they went into the hospital or stayed home from church because they were ill. What people don't realize is that when ministers graduate from seminary, we get a diploma—not powers of omniscience; not even a crystal ball.

I want to be the best pastor I can be, but pastors cannot offer pastoral care if the person or family doesn't let us know what's going on.

Think about it:

Have you ever misjudged a family member or friend for not calling or caring only to find out later that they didn't know what was going on? Has anyone ever misjudged you for not calling or caring—when *you* had no idea what was going on?

A good rule of thumb is to never assume someone knows something if you yourself didn't tell him directly.

Prayer:

Holy God, may I never judge another for not caring if they don't know what is happening to me. Amen.

Audrey Alexander

— Reflection #43: ————————————

During the holidays, society deems it socially inappropriate to be sad. The decorations, music, and the "we-must-get-together-during-the-holidays-and-gorge-ourselves" parties simply demand we "be happy."

But there are times, especially during the holidays, that the pain of loss comes to the forefront of our emotions. Other acute times are anniversaries of loss…and if those fall on a holiday, the pain is even worse.

Psychologists and behavioral therapists tell us that smiling and laughing—even when you don't feel like it—are helpful in lifting our spirits. I totally agree. What I would add are two subpoints. 1) It is indeed inappropriate to go to a party and mope—and expect everyone to join in moping with you. That's self-centered. But it does not mean you must deny or diminish the sadness you are feeling. Emotions demand to be heard; emotions left unacknowledged manifest in either a more depressed emotional state, or as a physical ailment. Do not ignore your emotions, especially the sad ones. Acknowledge them; share them with a friend. Cry if you want to. But don't let the sadness devolve. In the midst of those feelings, find *something* to smile about. Something, *anything,* to smile about will help you keep your psyche in balance. 2) The second subpoint is a reminder that happy-happy is not the same as joy. Joy is experiencing the presence of God no matter what the situation. Joy is not dependent on external circumstances. Joy—the presence of God—resides deep within us. That's why we can still sing and give gifts even if the pain of sadness and loss feels raw. Joy and sadness are not incompatible; happy-happy and sadness are. Happy-happy is a surface emotion triggered by external events—a party, a chocolate cupcake, a present…. But once the party is over, the cupcake eaten, and the present opened, happy-happy moments flutter away.

Joy is experiencing the presence of God in the moment, no matter what is happening around you.

Think about it:

The word "Emmanuel" is Greek for "God-with-us." God is with us, within us, around us always and forever. Joy is not just a whole bunch of "happy." Joy comes when we connect with Emmanuel, when we connect with the presence of God. Joy does not ignore or diminish the pain of loss and sadness; rather, joy transcends loss and sadness. That's the power of the divine Presence.

Prayer:

Holy God, help me experience your presence in a deeper way, especially when the pain of loss and sadness seems so sharp. Touch me in a way that opens me to taste moments of joy in the midst of grief. Amen.

— Reflection #44:

The second worst year of my life was 7th grade. I was verbally picked on, but I didn't fight back because I was taught fighting was wrong. I didn't tell my parents because it was too embarrassing, and if they had talked with the teacher or principal, it would have made life worse. My homework was stolen, and occasionally I just handed it over so I wouldn't get beat up. I was terrible at sports, and I wasn't an attractive 12-year-old. Every day when I walked to school, I repeated a mantra: "If I can get through this, I can get through anything." I said that from the time I left my home to the time I walked through the school doors. Seventh grade was humiliating, and there was nothing I could do about it.

Think about it:

All of us have horrible times in our lives. But we survived! If nothing else good came from those times, we can look back and say, "If I survived that, then I can survive this!" All of us are survivors, and that's something we can celebrate and recall to keep life in perspective. Good for you for surviving whatever time in your life was "7th grade."

But some people are so scarred from past traumas that they can't learn from it or move on from it. They perpetually live in "7th grade humiliation." And there are some people with mental illness that keep them trapped in "7th grade horror." People who cannot move on—people who cannot escape the "7th grade"—do not act normal and often are not nice to be around. Those "bums" on the street—the ones who "ought to get a job"—often cannot get a job (or keep a job) because something in their lives messed up how they are able to function. They live in humiliation.

Sometimes people live in humiliation because of abusive spouses, or abusive bosses, or from the memories of growing up in an abusive family…and we may never understand why they are unhappy or grouchy or critical or even mean.

What is the best way to relate to people who are hurting?

Prayer:

Holy God, help me be understanding and compassionate to those who, for whatever reason, live in humiliation and fear. Amen.

— Reflection #45:

What is the craziest New Year's resolution you ever made? One year I resolved to become ambidextrous. With the exception of signing my signature, I would do everything with my left hand until I became proficient at left-handedness.

This resolution lasted for slightly less than two weeks... which was 12 days longer than my resolution to quit eating fast food!

Another year I resolved to read the classics. I bought a paperback *unabridged* edition of *Les Miserables*. That thing is about nine thousand pages long! (Or so it felt like.) I **love** the story of *Les Miserables*, and for the record, I did finish reading the entire *unabridged* tome. The resolution ended after it took me three months to get through one book.

Think about it:

This is a just for fun "think about it": What's the craziest resolution you ever made? Why did you make it? Did you keep it? If not, why not?

Prayer:

Holy God, help me choose resolutions wisely. Amen.

— Reflection #46: ———————

Most of us will not win a Nobel Peace Prize; most of us will not be even a footnote in the history books. But that doesn't mean we are nobodies. We all make a difference. Julia Butterfly Hill said, "The question is not *can* you make a difference; you already *do* make a difference. It's just a matter of what kind of difference you want to make during your life on this planet."

Think about it:

Julia Butterfly Hill's quote is profound. You <u>are</u> making a difference in this world. The question is what difference are you making? If you are a parent, you can make an immeasurable difference for the good by spending both quality and quantity time with your children.

If you take the bus to work, you can make a difference by being polite to the driver and other passengers. This may be difficult, but you never know which of them will "pay it forward" and make the world a better place.

Evaluate your job. Is where you work making this world a better place? Sometimes we take and keep jobs because of the salary and benefits. When you've got a family to feed, I understand that. I do not judge. But look carefully at what your place of work is doing, especially if it is a large corporation. How is the place you work at helping the world; how is it hurting the world?

Do your best at whatever job you have, even if it's flipping burgers in a fast food restaurant. Doing your best at even the most seemingly insignificant task will make the world that much better. Maybe—probably—you won't see the effect your positive energy has. Not to worry. Transformation is happening on an energetic level, and over time, with enough people doing their best, extraordinary things can happen for the better.

"The question is not *can* you make a difference; you already *do* make a difference. It's just a matter of what kind of difference you want to make during your life on this planet."

Prayer:

Holy God, help me to make a difference for the better every day. Amen.

— Reflection #47: ————————

My mother said that education is never wasted. She's right. In college, I learned to drink a can of beer standing on my head. (I could do only about a fourth of a can, but it's still impressive.) I learned how to write a paper for my English Lit class, comparing the writing styles of two authors—without ever having read *any* of the assigned books. (That's not the lesson the professor intended.) (I got a B on the paper.) And I learned in a philosophy class that this guy named Jeremy Bentham put in his will that after his death, his body was to be stuffed and set out for public display. Sure enough, some college in London acquired the body of Bentham, and it's on public display except for special meetings when it is brought into the board room. Bentham is considered "present but not voting."

Mom just shook her head when I told her what I was learning in college. Nonetheless, she's right. Education is never wasted. My dad told me when I first started my freshman year that college is not about learning information and facts; it's about learning how to learn. He's right.

The skill of learning how to learn is never wasted. Thirty years after college, I doubt I could pass a 101 course in any of my majors. But even though specific facts have been forgotten, four years of "learning how to learn" has served me well. I learned how to think. That's not always obvious to my friends, but when I try real hard, I can think. That's a much better skill than mere memorization of facts.

And as it turns out, my unmarketable degrees of psychology, sociology, and philosophy turned out to be an excellent foundation for seminary. Yep, mom and dad were right.

Think about it:

How about signing up for a community college class? If that is not possible, then how about reading a book on a subject you have never explored and know nothing about? Even if you don't retain any specific information from the class or the book, your horizons will have broadened...and that's always a good thing. Education is never wasted.

Prayer:

Holy God, help me honor you with my mind as well as my heart. Amen.

— Reflection #48:

In seminary there were some courses I really struggled with. All tests in seminary were written essays (with the exception of two or three oral examinations). On one particular test, I had no clue what the answer was. So I crossed off that question and wrote my own question…and proceeded to write an essay on a question I knew the answer to. The professor was not amused. I got no credit.

I don't understand why. When James T. Kirk was taking a test to become captain of the Star Ship Enterprise, he realized that the test was rigged. The test was to pilot a simulated Star Ship, but Kirk figured out that whatever decision he made would result in destruction. So Kirk reprogrammed the computer so that he could land the Star Ship safely. The board of captain-choosers passed him!

So I ask you: what's the difference between reprogramming a simulated space ship to become a captain and writing my own essay question so I can become a pastor? None that I can see. And that wasn't the first time I learned life's not fair.

Think about it:

What situation in your life feels like a lose-lose? What would have to change for an acceptable outcome to occur? Do you have the ability to enact such a change? Sometimes change does not occur because we *can't* do anything differently; sometimes change does not occur because we *don't* do anything differently. Take another look at your situation and see if there *is* something you can do that you haven't thought of before. Maybe there isn't, but until you exhaust all possibilities, you'll never know.

Prayer:

Holy God, help me think outside the box so I can enact some change for the better. Amen.

— Reflection #49: —

When I was in high school, my parents insisted I take four years of math and four years of English because it would look good on my transcripts. The four years of English was no problem. But after one semester of freshman algebra, I was lost. It wasn't that I didn't try; it's more like I don't have "math synapses" in my brain.

Anyway, it was during the torturous year of trigonometry. The teacher told the class to do Problem #7. So I worked on it and came up with an answer. I looked around, and all the smart kids were still working. Not a good sign. Finally I got up the guts to raise my hand. What did I have to lose? It wouldn't be the first time I gave a wrong answer in class.

The teacher called on me, and I gave my answer. TA-DA!! I had the right answer! Will wonders never cease!

My best friend sat behind me; she was (is) good at math. She tapped me on the shoulder and whispered, "Let me see how you did that." After a moment, she whispered, "Well, I don't believe it." She whispered, "You did the wrong problem! You did Problem #8. And you did Problem #8 incorrectly. But your wrong answer to the wrong problem just *happened* to be the right answer to Problem #7!"

I whispered back, "What's your point? I got the answer the teacher wanted, and you didn't! Hee! Hee! Hee!"

Think about it:

The point of this reflection is not that two wrongs make a right! The point is that sometimes we get lucky. Usually, though, we remember and focus on the times we felt unlucky. Become mindful of the times something goes unexpectedly well, and *remember* those times.

I've heard many, many people say, "I'm never lucky." Of course you are lucky! You just have to notice and remember the times that things went right. Once you become mindful and notice even the littlest of things that went well, you'll realize just how lucky you really are.

Prayer:

Holy God, help me become mindful of all that is good and right in my life. Help me focus on what is right in a situation instead of what is wrong. Amen.

— Reflection #50: ————————

Who do you consider to be your best friend? What makes that person your best friend? Growing up, I had some very good friends. And then something disturbing and unfortunate happened. What surprised me was who stood by my side even though they didn't know the whole story. They still stood by me. It also surprised me who walked away from me.

I have never been angry at those who walked away. To this day, I continue to lift them in prayer and pray for their highest good. I trust that some day, if not in this life, then in the next, they will understand.

What touches my heart is the faithfulness of those who stood by me and did not judge. Those persons are truly "my best friends."

Think about it:

Have you ever had a friend walk away from you? Have you ever walked away from a friend? Who remained by your side when the going got tough? The Apostle Paul says in First Corinthians 13:12: *Now we see but a poor reflection as in a mirror; then we shall see face to face. Now I know in part; then I shall know fully…(NIV).* In other words, in this life, we are not capable of knowing the whole story; only in the next life will we fully understand. There are some writings of the Apostle Paul with which I disagree. I think he hit the nail on the head here. I hope and trust this is true.

Prayer:

Holy God, keep me from judging others because I am not capable of knowing the whole story about anything. And when others judge me, help me remember that some day, they will understand fully. Amen.

— Reflection #51: ————————————

When I was four or five years old, St. Louis had *The Showboat* on the riverfront. *The Showboat* was an old-fashioned river boat that offered melodramas—complete with villain, hero, and maiden-in-distress. My parents and a group of their friends went to see a show, and I went along.

I sat on the aisle seat so that I could lean out and see the stage. At the beginning of the show, the villain, dressed in black with a handlebar mustache, came from the back, down the aisle. I smiled at him. He stopped at my seat, raised his arms and shouted, "BOO-OO-OO" at me. I laughed. So he said something else to scare me (don't remember what exactly), and I clapped my hands and laughed. Finally he got down on one knee in the aisle, took his hat off, held it over his heart and said, "Please, kid, please be scared. I'll lose my job as the villain if you don't get scared!" By this time I was doing belly-laughs at him, practically falling out of my seat laughing. I don't remember what he did next, but the show went on. I think I waved to him once or twice while he was tying the maiden-in-distress to the railroad tracks.

Think about it:

Do you feel intimidated by anyone? Why do you think that is? Fear of judgment from them? Fear that you aren't as good at something as they are? Intimidation hinders us from doing our best, and *so what* if someone is better at something than you are! So what!

And you cannot control whether someone is going to judge you; that's not your karma. If someone is going to judge you, then excelling at something isn't really going to help; they'll find something else to judge you for. So you can't let fear of judgment thwart your best efforts.

Sometimes, as in the reflection above, laughing at the situation, instead of being scared, defuses the situation, and by extension, eliminates intimidation. You'd be surprised how many handlebar-mustached villains are not scary once you get to know them.

There are a handful of things that intimidate me, so it's unrealistic to expect that nothing in life will ever intimidate you again. But learning to laugh and say so what if I'm not great at this or that will certainly help us keep a healthier perspective.

Prayer:

Holy God, help me to do my best and not be intimidated by fear or handlebar mustaches. Amen.

— Reflection #52: ———————

Don't know where, but somewhere I read that more people would rather be right than be happy. Hmmm.

Think about it:

If being right and being happy were mutually exclusive, would you rather be right your whole life or happy your whole life? If you could divvy up percentage-wise how much you'd like to be right and how much you'd like to be happy, what would you choose? 50-50? 75-25?

If it meant repairing a relationship, would you tell the other "you're right" even though you know *you* are right? Is repairing a relationship more important than being right?

In Greek mythology, there is a goddess named Cassandra. She has the gift of prophecy, of always being right about what is going to happen; but the god Apollo curses her so that no one ever believes her. Now that's got to be frustrating!

Would you rather be right, but no one believe you, or would you rather be wrong sometimes and have to admit it?

While the above questions are rhetorical, their tentacles reach into real life. Relationships are damaged because "being right" is more important than "being happy" to most people. There are times when asserting that we are right may have merit: "Honey, we really CANNOT afford a bigger house" may be an instance when we'd want to advocate our position because of unhealthy future consequences to the budget if we don't. OK, there are situations in which "I'm right" is appropriate.

But do you really need to threaten the relationship because you are right that the ice cube tray wasn't filled properly? that the shortest route to Pizza Hut would have been to turn left instead of going straight? that *The Mentalist* is a better detective than *Monk*?

What if you had only five "I'M RIGHT" cards that you could use throughout your lifetime? Think about that the next time you feel ready to do battle because "you're right." Would you want to play one of your five cards on the issue? This is a good way to gain awareness of which battles are worth fighting and which are worth letting go. It's a good way to decide if the issue is worth risking happiness over.

Prayer:

Holy God, only you are right all of the time. Help me remember that. Amen.